Bangladesh in Crisis: The Fall of Democracy in 2024

How Election Fraud, Student Uprisings, and Military Actions Shaped a Nation's Future

Kashan Ajmeri

www.kashanajmeri.com

Chapter 1: Prelude to a Crisis: Political Tensions Before 2024

In the years leading up to 2024, Bangladesh found itself teetering on the edge of a political precipice. The country, once heralded for its economic growth and strides in human development, was now mired in deepening political discord. The roots of this crisis were not born overnight but were the culmination of years of escalating tensions, systemic issues, and increasingly autocratic governance under the leadership of Prime Minister Sheikh Hasina.

The Dominance of the Awami League
Sheikh Hasina's Awami League had been in power for over a decade, securing consecutive electoral victories since 2009. While these victories were touted as evidence of the party's enduring popularity, they were marred by allegations of vote rigging, suppression of opposition, and misuse of state resources.

The 2018 general election, in particular, raised serious concerns. Reports of voter intimidation, ballot stuffing, and the arrest of opposition leaders painted a troubling picture of Bangladesh's democratic health.

As the Awami League consolidated power, the space for dissent narrowed. Civil society, once a vibrant force in Bangladesh's political landscape, found itself under increasing pressure. Independent media faced censorship and intimidation, with several journalists and activists arrested on charges that critics claimed were politically motivated. The Digital Security Act, passed in 2018, became a tool for the government to silence dissenting voices under the guise of combating cybercrime.

Erosion of Democratic Institutions

The erosion of democratic institutions was another key factor in the growing political tensions.

The judiciary, which should have acted as a check on executive power, was perceived as being increasingly subservient to the government. High-profile cases against opposition leaders often resulted in swift convictions, raising questions about judicial independence. The Election Commission, tasked with ensuring free and fair elections, was also accused of being biased in favor of the ruling party, further undermining public confidence in the electoral process.

The opposition, primarily the Bangladesh Nationalist Party (BNP), struggled to mount an effective challenge. Beset by internal divisions and leadership crises, the BNP found itself unable to mobilize significant public support. The party's repeated boycotts of elections only served to weaken its position further, leaving the political arena largely dominated by the Awami League.

Economic Discontent and Social Inequality

While Bangladesh's economy had grown steadily over the years, this growth was not evenly distributed. Wealth inequality widened, and the benefits of economic progress were increasingly concentrated in the hands of a few. Corruption, cronyism, and nepotism became rampant, with powerful elites controlling vast swathes of the economy. For the average Bangladeshi, life remained a daily struggle, with rising costs of living, unemployment, and inadequate public services fueling discontent.

Rural areas, in particular, felt neglected, as government development projects were often concentrated in urban centers. The agrarian sector, still a significant part of the economy, suffered from lack of investment and support. Farmers, burdened by debt and low crop prices, were among the most vocal in their dissatisfaction.

The Role of Students in Political Activism

Students have historically played a crucial role in Bangladesh's political movements, and the years leading up to 2024 were no exception. The discontent among the youth was palpable, driven by unemployment, corruption in educational institutions, and a lack of opportunities. The 2018 road safety protests, sparked by the death of two students in a traffic accident, showcased the power of student activism. What began as a call for safer roads quickly morphed into a broader critique of government incompetence and corruption.

The government's heavy-handed response to these protests, including the use of tear gas, rubber bullets, and mass arrests, only served to galvanize the students further. Social media became a battleground, with students using it to organize and disseminate information, despite government attempts to curtail online freedom.

Rising Religious Tensions

Religious tensions also simmered beneath the surface, exacerbated by the government's perceived favoritism towards certain groups. While Bangladesh is constitutionally a secular state, the rise of Islamist groups and the government's ambiguous stance on secularism versus religious identity created a volatile environment. Attacks on religious minorities, bloggers, and secular activists became more frequent, raising concerns about the country's commitment to religious tolerance.

The Countdown to 2024

As 2024 approached, these various threads of discontent began to intertwine, creating a perfect storm. The government, rather than addressing the root causes of these issues, doubled down on its authoritarian measures.

The stage was set for a major confrontation, with the country deeply divided and its democratic institutions weakened. The elections of 2024, rather than being a resolution of these tensions, would become the catalyst for an unprecedented crisis, the effects of which would ripple across the nation and beyond.

This chapter lays the foundation for understanding how Bangladesh, a country with so much potential, found itself on the brink of political disaster. The seeds of the crisis were sown over many years, with each passing event contributing to the eventual collapse of the democratic facade. As we move forward in this book, the full scope of the 2024 crisis will be explored, but it is crucial to understand that this was a crisis long in the making, with deep roots in the political and social fabric of Bangladesh.

Chapter 2: The Rigged Election
Unraveling the Fraud

The 2024 general election in Bangladesh will be remembered not for the exercise of democracy but for its blatant manipulation. What was supposed to be a democratic process became an orchestrated charade, where the outcome seemed pre-determined long before the first vote was cast. This chapter uncovers the layers of deception, corruption, and coercion that marred the election, exposing how the ruling Awami League undermined the very foundation of Bangladesh's democracy.

Pre-Election Strategies: Setting the Stage for Fraud

Months before the election, the ruling Awami League began to lay the groundwork for an outcome in their favor.

The first step was ensuring that key opposition leaders could not participate effectively. The government employed a strategy of "lawfare," using the judiciary to disqualify candidates from opposition parties, most notably the Bangladesh Nationalist Party (BNP). Court cases against opposition figures, many based on weak or fabricated evidence, resulted in convictions or legal battles that barred them from running.

The Election Commission, expected to be an impartial guardian of the democratic process, was far from independent. Appointments to the Commission were strategically made to ensure loyalty to the ruling party. Reports of voter roll tampering, biased decisions, and outright dismissals of legitimate complaints from the opposition parties indicated that the Commission was more interested in facilitating the Awami League's victory than ensuring a fair election.

The Role of State Institutions: A Systematic Undermining of Democracy

State institutions, which should have acted as checks on executive power, were instead co-opted to serve the ruling party's agenda. The police, intelligence services, and administrative machinery were all used to intimidate and suppress opposition activities. Opposition rallies were routinely disrupted under the guise of maintaining public order, while pro-government gatherings were given full protection.

Election day itself was marred by widespread irregularities. Reports emerged of ballot boxes being stuffed with votes for the Awami League before polling stations even opened. Polling agents from opposition parties were often denied access to polling stations, leaving the government's agents free to manipulate the process.

Voters faced intimidation at polling stations, with many reporting that they were pressured or coerced into voting for the ruling party.

Media Control and Propaganda: Shaping Public Perception

The media played a crucial role in shaping public perception leading up to the election. Over the years, the government had tightened its grip on both traditional and digital media. Independent news outlets were systematically weakened, either through financial pressure, legal challenges, or direct threats to journalists. Those that remained operational were careful in their reporting, avoiding any coverage that could be seen as critical of the government.

State-controlled media and pro-government outlets, on the other hand, were unleashed in full force.

A constant stream of propaganda painted the Awami League as the only viable option for stability and progress, while the opposition was depicted as corrupt and chaotic. During the election campaign, state media gave overwhelming coverage to Awami League candidates while sidelining the opposition. Social media, once a platform for dissent and organization, was heavily monitored and censored, with pro-government content flooding platforms to drown out dissenting voices.

The Voting Process: A Day of Deception
On the day of the election, the extent of the fraud became fully apparent. Observers reported numerous incidents of pre-filled ballots, where boxes were stuffed in favor of the Awami League before voting even began. Opposition polling agents, who are supposed to be present to ensure transparency, were often barred from entering polling stations or were forced out by intimidation tactics.

In rural areas, where oversight was even weaker, entire communities reported being coerced into voting for the ruling party under threat of reprisal.

In urban centers, where the opposition had traditionally held more sway, tactics were slightly different. Long delays at polling stations, unexplained technical issues with voting machines, and a sudden surge of votes for the Awami League in the final hours of voting raised serious doubts about the legitimacy of the process. Despite widespread allegations of fraud, the Election Commission quickly certified the results, declaring a landslide victory for the Awami League.

The Aftermath: A Nation in Turmoil

The immediate aftermath of the election was marked by disbelief, outrage, and protest. The opposition, alongside civil society groups and international observers, condemned the election as a farce. Protests erupted across the country, particularly in Dhaka, where students and activists took to the streets to decry the stolen election. The government's response was swift and brutal. Security forces were deployed to suppress the protests, leading to violent clashes and numerous casualties.

Despite the outcry, the Awami League moved quickly to consolidate its power. The newly formed government dismissed calls for an investigation into the election, insisting that the results reflected the will of the people. With the opposition in disarray and the media muzzled, the ruling party tightened its grip on power, leaving little room for dissent.

International Reaction: Condemnation and Silence

International reaction to the election was mixed. While some countries and international organizations condemned the process and called for a new election, others were more muted in their response, wary of jeopardizing strategic relationships with Bangladesh. The government's swift moves to quell dissent and secure diplomatic support further isolated the opposition and stifled any hopes of immediate redress.

The 2024 election marked a significant turning point in Bangladesh's political history. What should have been a democratic process became a symbol of authoritarian control. The events surrounding this election set the stage for the widespread unrest and turmoil that would follow, as the people of Bangladesh struggled to reclaim their democracy from those who had so thoroughly corrupted it.

In this chapter, we've unraveled the complex web of actions and decisions that led to the rigged 2024 election. From the manipulation of state institutions to the suppression of dissenting voices, it's clear that the election was not just a failure of democracy—it was a calculated and deliberate effort to undermine it. The consequences of this fraudulent election would ripple through Bangladesh, igniting the crisis that this book seeks to explore in detail.

Chapter 3: Voices Silenced: Media Control and Opposition Suppression

In the years leading up to the 2024 crisis, Bangladesh witnessed an unprecedented crackdown on freedom of expression. The government, led by Sheikh Hasina and the Awami League, understood the power of information in shaping public opinion and controlling the narrative. To ensure their hold on power, they embarked on a systematic campaign to suppress the opposition and silence the media. This chapter delves into the mechanisms of media control and the suppression of dissent, which played a pivotal role in the erosion of democracy in Bangladesh.

The Stranglehold on Independent Media
Independent media in Bangladesh had long been a thorn in the side of the ruling party.

For decades, journalists, editors, and media houses had provided a critical check on government power, exposing corruption, mismanagement, and human rights abuses. However, as the 2024 election approached, the environment for independent journalism became increasingly hostile.

The government employed a variety of tactics to stifle independent voices. Financial pressure was one of the most effective tools in its arsenal. Media outlets that dared to criticize the government found themselves facing a sudden loss of advertising revenue, often due to pressure exerted on businesses by government officials. In some cases, tax audits and legal challenges were used to drain the financial resources of media houses, forcing many to either shut down or tow the government line.

Censorship became more overt as well. The government routinely issued directives to media outlets, instructing them on what could and could not be reported. Sensitive topics, such as electoral fraud, human rights abuses, or criticism of the Prime Minister, were off-limits. Failure to comply often resulted in swift retribution, including arrests of editors or shutdowns of entire news organizations.

The Digital Security Act, passed in 2018, became a key weapon in the government's arsenal. Ostensibly designed to combat cybercrime, the law was used to target journalists, bloggers, and social media activists who voiced dissenting opinions. Under this law, numerous journalists were arrested on charges of "spreading rumors" or "hurting religious sentiments," charges that were often vague and politically motivated. The threat of arrest or legal action created a climate of fear, leading many journalists to self-censor or avoid controversial topics altogether.

State-Controlled Media: The Propaganda Machine

As independent voices were silenced, state-controlled media and pro-government outlets filled the vacuum. These outlets became the primary source of news for much of the population, disseminating a narrative that was heavily skewed in favor of the ruling party. The government's control over state media allowed it to shape public perception, particularly in rural areas where access to diverse sources of information was limited.

State media portrayed the government as a benevolent force, dedicated to development and progress, while the opposition was depicted as corrupt, violent, and unfit to govern. This relentless stream of propaganda not only bolstered the ruling party's image but also deepened divisions within the country, as those who relied solely on state media.

Were often unaware of the growing discontent and the legitimate grievances of the opposition.

Crackdown on Opposition Voices
Beyond the media, the government also targeted opposition parties and leaders, ensuring that they had little to no platform from which to challenge the ruling party's narrative. The Bangladesh Nationalist Party (BNP) and other opposition groups faced severe restrictions on their activities. Their rallies were frequently disrupted by police, permits for public gatherings were denied, and party offices were raided.

Key opposition leaders were systematically targeted with legal cases, often based on flimsy or fabricated charges. High-profile figures like BNP leader Khaleda Zia were imprisoned on corruption charges widely seen as politically motivated. These legal battles drained the resources of opposition parties and diverted their focus away from election campaigning.

Social media, which had emerged as a potent tool for organizing and dissent, was also tightly controlled. The government increased surveillance of online activities, with special units established to monitor social media platforms. Activists and opposition supporters found themselves targeted for online posts that criticized the government, leading to arrests and harassment. Internet shutdowns and throttling of social media platforms became common tactics during periods of heightened tension, particularly in the run-up to the election.

The International Community's Tepid Response

Despite the clear suppression of media freedom and political opposition, the international community's response was largely muted. While some human rights organizations and a few Western governments issued statements of concern, these were often overshadowed by geopolitical considerations.

Bangladesh's strategic importance in the region, coupled with its role as a major contributor to international peacekeeping forces, meant that many countries were reluctant to press too hard on issues of democracy and human rights.

The government's ability to maintain a facade of economic progress also played a role in tempering international criticism. With the economy continuing to grow and poverty rates declining, the narrative of Bangladesh as a development success story remained appealing to many international partners, who were wary of destabilizing a key ally in a volatile region.

The Consequences of Suppression

The suppression of media and opposition voices had profound consequences for Bangladesh. The lack of a free and independent press meant that corruption and abuses of power went largely unchecked.

The public, deprived of accurate information, was unable to make informed decisions, leading to a growing disconnect between the government and the governed.

The silencing of the opposition created an atmosphere of frustration and resentment. With no legitimate avenues for political expression, many opposition supporters turned to more radical means of protest. The government's heavy-handed approach to dissent only fueled further unrest, setting the stage for the widespread protests and violence that would erupt in the wake of the 2024 election.

In this chapter, we've examined how the systematic suppression of media and opposition voices played a crucial role in the unraveling of democracy in Bangladesh.

The erosion of these fundamental pillars of a free society not only allowed the ruling party to maintain its grip on power but also contributed to the deepening crisis that would soon engulf the nation. As we move forward, the impact of these actions will become increasingly clear, as the people of Bangladesh rise up to reclaim their voice and their democracy.

Chapter 4: Student Uprising: The Youth Lead the Charge

The student uprising in Bangladesh was a critical turning point in the nation's unfolding political crisis. As discontent simmered across the country, it was the youth—disillusioned, frustrated, and determined—who became the catalyst for widespread resistance against the government. This chapter explores the origins, motivations, and impact of the student-led protests that shook Bangladesh in 2024.

The Roots of Discontent

The seeds of the student uprising were sown years before the 2024 election. Bangladesh's young population had grown increasingly frustrated with the government's failures on several fronts. Despite the country's economic growth, youth unemployment remained stubbornly high, leaving many graduates without meaningful job prospects. Corruption within educational institutions further exacerbated the sense of injustice.

Students faced bribery, nepotism, and political interference in admissions, grading, and job placements, making meritocracy seem like a distant dream.

Another major source of frustration was the quota system in government jobs. Originally designed to provide opportunities for marginalized groups, the system had become deeply unpopular among students, who felt it was unfairly limiting their chances of securing employment based on merit. Protests against the quota system in 2018 had already highlighted the growing unrest among students, but these earlier movements were just the beginning.

By 2024, the students' dissatisfaction had reached a boiling point. The rigged election, combined with the government's increasingly authoritarian measures, convinced many young people that their future was being stolen by a corrupt and unaccountable regime.

The Spark of Rebellion

The tipping point for the student uprising came in the form of widespread allegations of electoral fraud in the 2024 election. The blatant manipulation of the voting process, coupled with the silencing of opposition voices, outraged students who had hoped for a change in leadership. For many, the election was the final proof that the democratic process in Bangladesh was fundamentally broken.

What began as small gatherings of students expressing their anger and frustration soon grew into large-scale protests. Universities and colleges across the country became hotbeds of resistance, with students organizing rallies, sit-ins, and marches demanding justice, transparency, and a return to true democratic governance. Social media played a crucial role in mobilizing students and spreading the message of resistance.

Platforms like Facebook and Twitter became hubs of activism, where students shared information, coordinated actions, and called for solidarity. Despite government efforts to monitor and censor online activity, the youth's tech-savviness allowed them to stay one step ahead, using encrypted messaging apps and other tools to evade surveillance.

The Government's Response: Repression and Violence

The government's response to the student protests was swift and brutal. Security forces were deployed to quell the demonstrations, and what began as peaceful protests quickly escalated into violent confrontations. Riot police used tear gas, rubber bullets, and batons to disperse crowds, leading to numerous injuries and, in some cases, deaths.

The crackdown only fueled the students' anger and determination. Rather than being intimidated into submission, the violence served to galvanize the movement. The protests spread beyond university campuses, drawing in citizens from all walks of life who were sympathetic to the students' cause. In cities like Dhaka, Chittagong, and Sylhet, mass protests brought daily life to a standstill, as thousands took to the streets to demand change.

The government also attempted to weaken the movement by targeting its leaders. Student activists were arrested, often in the dead of night, and subjected to harsh interrogations. Some were charged under the Digital Security Act for "inciting unrest" or "spreading misinformation," while others were simply detained without charge, their whereabouts unknown for days or even weeks.

The Role of Universities and Educational Institutions

Universities and colleges became both the physical and symbolic battlegrounds of the student uprising. These institutions, traditionally seen as centers of learning and intellectual development, were transformed into hubs of resistance. Lecture halls and campuses became venues for organizing, where students debated strategy, crafted slogans, and prepared for the next protest.

However, these spaces were also heavily policed. University administrations, many of whom were under pressure from the government, often sided with the authorities, implementing measures to control student activities. Some institutions imposed curfews, shut down campuses, or even called in police to disperse gatherings.

Despite these challenges, students found creative ways to continue their activism. They held underground meetings, distributed pamphlets, and used guerrilla tactics to outmaneuver the authorities. The resilience and adaptability of the student movement became a hallmark of their struggle, inspiring others to join the cause.

The Broader Impact: Awakening a Nation

The student uprising had a profound impact on Bangladesh's political landscape. It not only highlighted the deep-seated grievances of the country's youth but also acted as a catalyst for broader societal unrest. The courage and determination of the students resonated with many ordinary citizens who had grown disillusioned with the status quo.

As the protests continued, they began to attract support from other segments of society.

Labor unions, professional organizations, and civil society groups expressed solidarity with the students, organizing their own demonstrations and strikes. The movement began to take on a life of its own, evolving from a student protest into a nationwide call for change.

The government's attempts to portray the students as unruly agitators failed to resonate with a public that saw through the propaganda. Instead, the students were increasingly viewed as heroes, standing up for the rights and freedoms of all Bangladeshis. Their actions inspired a wave of activism across the country, as more and more people found the courage to speak out against the government's abuses.

The Legacy of the Uprising

The student uprising of 2024 marked a turning point in Bangladesh's history. It was a powerful demonstration of the potential for youth-led movements to challenge authoritarian regimes and demand accountability. While the immediate outcomes of the uprising were still uncertain, its impact on the country's political consciousness was undeniable.

In the following chapters, we will explore how this wave of activism interacted with other forces in Bangladesh, leading to the unfolding crisis. The students, though young and often dismissed by the authorities as inexperienced, had shown that they were a force to be reckoned with—a force that would not be silenced, no matter the cost. The legacy of their struggle would continue to shape the nation's future, as Bangladesh grappled with the consequences of its stolen democracy.

Chapter 5: Violence in the Streets: From Protests to Rebellion

As the student-led protests in Bangladesh gained momentum, what began as peaceful demonstrations rapidly escalated into widespread violence. The government's heavy-handed response to dissent—marked by brutal crackdowns, mass arrests, and a disregard for human rights—ignited a firestorm of anger and resentment across the country. This chapter delves into how the situation spiraled from peaceful protest to violent rebellion, examining the key events and decisions that fueled the escalation.

The Escalation of Violence

The initial protests were largely peaceful, with students demanding justice for the rigged election and an end to the authoritarian policies of Sheikh Hasina's government.

However, the government's aggressive crackdown—deploying police and paramilitary forces to disperse crowds with batons, tear gas, and rubber bullets—provoked widespread outrage. The sight of injured and bloodied students being dragged away by security forces was broadcasted across social media, sparking a wave of solidarity protests in cities and towns across Bangladesh.

In response to the violence, the protesters' tactics began to change. Initially armed with little more than slogans and placards, many students and activists began to fight back. Barricades were erected in city streets, and stones and makeshift weapons were used to fend off the advancing security forces. The government, in turn, escalated its response, deploying live ammunition and detaining thousands of protesters in an attempt to crush the burgeoning rebellion.

The Role of Paramilitary and Law Enforcement

The government's decision to involve elite paramilitary units, such as the Rapid Action Battalion (RAB), marked a significant turning point in the unrest. Known for their ruthless tactics, these forces were unleashed on the protesters with orders to restore order by any means necessary. Reports of extrajudicial killings, enforced disappearances, and severe torture began to emerge, deepening the sense of injustice and galvanizing further resistance.

In urban centers like Dhaka, Chittagong, and Rajshahi, the violence reached a fever pitch. Security forces patrolled the streets, enforcing curfews and engaging in running battles with protesters. Many neighborhoods became virtual war zones, with daily clashes between heavily armed security personnel and increasingly desperate protesters.

The Involvement of Militant Groups

As the violence intensified, radical elements began to infiltrate the movement. Militant groups, some with long-standing grievances against the government, saw the unrest as an opportunity to further their own agendas. These groups provided training, weapons, and strategic support to the protesters, transforming the movement into a more organized and dangerous rebellion.

The involvement of these militant factions further complicated the situation. While some protesters welcomed the support, others feared that the movement was losing its original purpose. The government, for its part, seized upon the presence of militants to justify even harsher measures, painting the entire movement as a terrorist insurrection rather than a legitimate political protest.

The Spread of Unrest to Rural Areas

Initially concentrated in urban centers, the rebellion soon spread to rural areas, where grievances against the government were equally, if not more, deeply rooted. Rural communities, particularly those in regions long neglected by the central government, joined the rebellion with fervor. The rural insurgents brought a new level of intensity to the conflict, using their knowledge of the terrain to launch guerrilla-style attacks on government forces.

The spread of unrest to the countryside marked a significant escalation, as the government found itself fighting on multiple fronts. The rebellion was no longer just a series of urban protests; it had become a nationwide insurrection, with pockets of resistance springing up across the country. Roads were blocked, government buildings were attacked, and local officials were forced to flee or face the wrath of the insurgents.

The Government's Descent into Desperation

As the rebellion grew, the government's actions became increasingly desperate and brutal. Widespread curfews, internet blackouts, and mass arrests became the norm. Security forces conducted raids on suspected rebel strongholds, often resulting in heavy civilian casualties. The death toll mounted daily, with bodies left in the streets as a grim reminder of the cost of defiance.

The government's attempts to crush the rebellion only fueled the cycle of violence. Each act of repression was met with more resistance, as the rebels grew more emboldened and the population more enraged. Reports of atrocities committed by security forces—such as the killing of unarmed civilians, the destruction of homes, and the torture of detainees—further alienated the public and eroded whatever remaining legitimacy the government had.

International Attention and Humanitarian Concerns

As the violence escalated, the international community began to take notice. Reports of human rights violations and the growing humanitarian crisis in Bangladesh prompted calls for intervention and mediation. However, the government, determined to maintain its hold on power, rejected outside interference, framing the rebellion as an internal matter.

Humanitarian organizations raised alarms about the deteriorating situation, particularly the plight of civilians caught in the crossfire. The conflict had led to widespread displacement, with thousands of people fleeing their homes in search of safety. Refugee camps sprang up along the borders, and neighboring countries began to brace for the possibility of a full-scale civil war.

The Beginning of a Full-Blown Rebellion

By the end of 2024, what had begun as a student-led protest had evolved into a full-scale rebellion. The streets of Bangladesh were no longer just sites of protest but battlegrounds in a fight for the country's future. The violence that had engulfed the nation showed no signs of abating, with both sides digging in for a prolonged struggle.

In this chapter, we have traced the descent from peaceful protests to violent rebellion, a process driven by government repression and the unyielding determination of a population that refused to be silenced. As Bangladesh plunged deeper into crisis, the lines between protest and rebellion blurred, setting the stage for the tumultuous events that would follow. The conflict had reached a point of no return, with the future of the nation hanging in the balance.

Chapter 6: From Protest to Revolt: The Escalation of Violence

The transition from peaceful protest to full-blown revolt in Bangladesh was a complex and multi-faceted process, marked by a series of escalating confrontations between the government and the people. This chapter explores the dynamics that fueled this escalation, tracing how the initial demands for justice transformed into a widespread revolt that shook the foundations of the nation.

The Triggering Events: From Peaceful Beginnings to Violent Reactions

The roots of the escalation can be traced to the government's heavy-handed response to the early protests. Initially, the demonstrations were peaceful, organized by students and civil society groups calling for electoral reform and an end to corruption.

The Beginning of a Full-Blown Rebellion

By the end of 2024, what had begun as a student-led protest had evolved into a full-scale rebellion. The streets of Bangladesh were no longer just sites of protest but battlegrounds in a fight for the country's future. The violence that had engulfed the nation showed no signs of abating, with both sides digging in for a prolonged struggle.

In this chapter, we have traced the descent from peaceful protests to violent rebellion, a process driven by government repression and the unyielding determination of a population that refused to be silenced. As Bangladesh plunged deeper into crisis, the lines between protest and rebellion blurred, setting the stage for the tumultuous events that would follow. The conflict had reached a point of no return, with the future of the nation hanging in the balance.

However, the government's refusal to engage in dialogue, coupled with its reliance on brute force to disperse protesters, led to a significant shift in the movement's tactics.

As security forces began using tear gas, rubber bullets, and live ammunition against unarmed protesters, the tone of the demonstrations changed. What had started as a peaceful call for reform quickly morphed into anger and defiance. The images of wounded and bloodied protesters, widely shared on social media, stoked the flames of resistance, drawing more people into the streets and radicalizing those who were already involved.

The Role of Government Repression

The government's strategy of repression only served to intensify the conflict. Mass arrests, beatings, and the use of lethal force against demonstrators became commonplace. The state's attempt to control the narrative through censorship and media crackdowns failed to suppress the truth; instead, it fueled resentment and deepened the divide between the government and the populace.

The arrests of key opposition leaders and activists further inflamed tensions. Many were detained without charges, held incommunicado, or subjected to harsh interrogations. This repression created a martyrdom effect, where those who were imprisoned or killed became symbols of resistance, inspiring others to take up the cause.

The Rise of Militant Factions

As the government's repression grew more intense, segments of the protest movement began to adopt more militant tactics. Initially focused on defensive actions, such as protecting protesters from police violence, these groups gradually took on a more offensive posture. Barricades, street battles, and attacks on government property became more frequent, signaling a shift from protest to armed revolt.

The influx of weapons and the emergence of armed factions within the movement marked a significant turning point. While the majority of protesters remained committed to non-violence, the presence of armed groups complicated the dynamics of the uprising. These factions often operated independently of the broader movement, pursuing their own agendas and sometimes clashing with other protesters.

The Spread of Violence Across the Country

The escalation of violence was not confined to the capital, Dhaka. As the revolt gained momentum, it spread to other cities and rural areas, each with its own unique set of grievances and dynamics. In some regions, local militias and tribal groups joined the revolt, bringing their own long-standing issues with the government into the broader conflict.

The rural areas, in particular, saw a rise in guerrilla-style warfare, with insurgent groups using hit-and-run tactics against government forces. These groups exploited the terrain and the government's lack of control over remote regions, launching attacks on military convoys, police stations, and government installations. The spread of violence to these areas further strained the government's resources and made it increasingly difficult to contain the revolt.

We Value Your Feedback!

Thank you for reading Bangladesh in Crisis: The Fall of Democracy in 2024. Your thoughts and opinions are important to us. Please take a moment to share your reviews and suggestions on Amazon. Your feedback helps us improve and reach more readers.

For updates on future books and exclusive content, visit our website: https://kashanajmeri.com/.

We look forward to hearing from you!

International Reactions and Involvement

The international community watched the unfolding crisis in Bangladesh with growing concern. Reports of human rights abuses and the scale of the violence drew condemnation from foreign governments and international organizations. Some countries imposed sanctions on the Bangladeshi government, while others offered to mediate the conflict. However, the government's refusal to accept foreign intervention and its determination to crush the revolt by force limited the impact of these efforts.

In some cases, foreign powers became indirectly involved in the conflict. Reports emerged of arms smuggling, with weapons flowing into the hands of rebel groups from neighboring countries. The complex web of regional geopolitics further complicated the situation, as external actors sought to influence the outcome of the conflict for their own strategic interests.

The Turning Point: A Nation at War

By the end of 2024, Bangladesh was in a state of de facto civil war. The government's attempts to suppress the revolt had only served to intensify it, and the violence showed no signs of abating. The country was deeply polarized, with entire communities divided along political lines. In some areas, local authorities had lost control entirely, and the rule of law had broken down.

The escalation from protest to revolt was not inevitable, but it was the result of a series of miscalculations and failures on both sides. The government's reliance on force, the radicalization of elements within the protest movement, and the involvement of external actors all contributed to the descent into violence. In this chapter, we have traced the trajectory of this escalation, highlighting the key events and decisions that transformed a peaceful protest movement into a nationwide revolt.

The consequences of this escalation would be felt for years to come, as Bangladesh struggled to rebuild in the aftermath of a conflict that had torn the nation apart.

Chapter 7: Sheikh Hasina's Last Stand: The Government's Response

As the nation teetered on the brink of collapse, Sheikh Hasina's government faced its most significant challenge yet. This chapter explores the strategies employed by the government in its desperate bid to maintain control, the internal divisions that emerged within the ruling party, and the consequences of the decisions made during this critical period.

Reasserting Authority Amid Chaos
In the wake of escalating violence and a growing revolt, Sheikh Hasina's government was determined to reassert its authority. The Prime Minister, known for her tenacity, framed the uprising as an existential threat to the nation's stability and sovereignty. In her public addresses, Hasina vowed to restore order, branding the protesters and opposition as "terrorists" and "enemies of the state.

" This rhetoric set the tone for the government's response, which was marked by an increasingly authoritarian approach.

Central to the government's strategy was a crackdown on dissent. The state apparatus—ranging from the police and military to intelligence agencies—was mobilized to suppress the revolt. Curfews were imposed in major cities, internet access was restricted, and a state of emergency was declared, granting the government sweeping powers to detain suspects without trial.

Consolidating Power: The Inner Circle's Role Behind the scenes, Hasina's inner circle played a crucial role in shaping the government's response. Key advisors and military leaders met frequently to discuss strategies for quelling the unrest.

The Military's Dual Role

While the military had initially taken a backseat, allowing police and paramilitary forces to handle the unrest, it became increasingly involved as the situation deteriorated. With the spread of violence to rural areas and the growing strength of militant factions within the protest movement, the government turned to the army for support. Military units were deployed in key hotspots, conducting operations against rebel strongholds and securing critical infrastructure.

However, the military's involvement was not without controversy. There were reports of human rights abuses, including extrajudicial killings and torture, which further alienated the population and fueled the rebellion. The military's actions, while intended to restore order, often had the opposite effect, driving more people into the arms of the opposition.

Internal Strife: The Cracks Begin to Show

As the crisis dragged on, internal divisions within the ruling party and government became more pronounced. Some senior members of the Awami League, Hasina's party, began to question the government's strategy. They feared that the hardline approach was pushing the country towards civil war and could ultimately lead to the collapse of the government.

These internal rifts were compounded by the deteriorating economy. The unrest had brought much of the country to a standstill, with businesses shuttered, supply chains disrupted, and investor confidence plummeting. The economic impact of the crisis added to the government's woes, eroding public support and creating a sense of desperation within the ruling elite.

Seeking International Support

Facing mounting pressure at home, Hasina's government sought to bolster its position by reaching out to international allies. Diplomatic efforts were made to secure support from key countries, including China and India, both of which had significant interests in Bangladesh. The government also appealed to the United Nations, framing the revolt as a security threat that required international intervention.

However, the international response was lukewarm. While some countries offered rhetorical support, there was little appetite for direct involvement in what was seen as an internal conflict. Moreover, reports of human rights abuses by the government's forces complicated efforts to garner international sympathy.

The Final Gambit: A Calculated Risk

As 2024 drew to a close, it became clear that the government's approach was not yielding the desired results. The rebellion had not been crushed, and the violence showed no signs of abating. In a last-ditch effort to regain control, Hasina made a calculated risk: she ordered a major military offensive against the strongest rebel-held areas.

This offensive, dubbed "Operation Iron Fist," was launched with the aim of delivering a decisive blow to the opposition. The government mobilized thousands of troops, supported by airstrikes and heavy artillery, in a concerted effort to reclaim territory and break the back of the rebellion. The operation was brutal, with significant casualties on both sides and widespread destruction.

The Aftermath: A Pyrrhic Victory

While "Operation Iron Fist" succeeded in retaking key areas and temporarily blunting the momentum of the rebellion, it came at a great cost. The offensive exacerbated the humanitarian crisis, displacing thousands of civilians and further deepening the country's divisions. The government had won a battle, but the war for the soul of Bangladesh was far from over.

In the aftermath of the operation, Hasina's government found itself in a precarious position. The revolt had been contained but not defeated, and the underlying grievances that had fueled the uprising remained unresolved. The government's legitimacy was severely undermined, and the country was left deeply scarred by the conflict.

This chapter has examined the government's response to the escalating crisis in Bangladesh, highlighting the strategies, decisions, and internal dynamics that shaped Sheikh Hasina's last stand. As the country emerged from this period of intense violence, it faced an uncertain future, with the specter of further unrest looming on the horizon.

Chapter 8: Military Intervention: The Army's Role and Actions

As Bangladesh's political crisis escalated, the military was thrust into the spotlight, forced to navigate a delicate balance between upholding the constitution and responding to the government's demands for control. This chapter delves into the army's role during the crisis, exploring the internal deliberations, the strategic deployments, and the actions taken by military leaders that would ultimately shape the outcome of the conflict.

The Military's Calculated Entry
The army's initial reluctance to intervene directly in the political turmoil was shaped by its historical role and the lessons learned from past interventions. Senior military officials were wary of the potential repercussions of taking sides in a highly polarized environment.

The military's primary objective was to maintain national stability, and any action had to be weighed against the risk of plunging the country further into chaos.

As violence spread across the country and the civilian government struggled to maintain control, pressure mounted on the military to act. The tipping point came when the scale of the rebellion reached levels that local police and paramilitary forces could no longer manage. The military's entry was gradual, beginning with logistical support and advisory roles, before escalating to full-scale operations in response to deteriorating conditions on the ground.

The military's actions were effective in reclaiming territory but came with significant collateral damage, including civilian casualties and the destruction of property.

Challenges and Internal Dissent

The military's intervention was not without challenges. Within the ranks, there was significant debate over the extent of the army's involvement. Some officers advocated for a more aggressive approach, pushing for the complete pacification of rebel-held areas, while others argued for restraint, fearing that excessive force could erode the military's public support and legitimacy.

This internal dissent reflected broader concerns about the military's long-term role in the conflict. The fear of being drawn into a protracted civil war weighed heavily on military leaders.

There was also the issue of loyalty within the ranks, as some soldiers and junior officers sympathized with the protesters' grievances, complicating the command structure and leading to instances of insubordination.

The Military's Relationship with the Government

The relationship between the military and Sheikh Hasina's government was complex and occasionally strained. While the government depended on the military to suppress the revolt, there were disagreements over strategy and the extent of the military's autonomy in decision-making. Some in the government viewed the military's growing power with suspicion, fearing that it could lead to a coup or a shift in the balance of power away from civilian rule. Despite these tensions, the military leadership maintained a public stance of loyalty to the government.

However, behind closed doors, there were discussions about the future of the nation and the possibility of a post-crisis transition. The military's ultimate goal was to restore order and stability, but there were growing concerns about the government's ability to govern effectively in the long term.

Consequences of Military Actions
The military's intervention had immediate and long-term consequences for Bangladesh. In the short term, the army's actions helped to contain the rebellion and restore a semblance of order in key areas. However, the heavy-handed tactics used by the military also exacerbated tensions and deepened the divide between the government and its opponents.

The widespread use of force alienated large segments of the population, particularly in regions that bore the brunt of military operations.

The destruction caused by the conflict, coupled with reports of human rights abuses, further eroded public trust in the government and the military. While the military succeeded in quelling the most immediate threats, the underlying causes of the rebellion remained unresolved, setting the stage for continued unrest.

The Aftermath: A Fragile Peace

As the military gradually scaled back its operations, the country was left in a state of fragile peace. The rebellion had been suppressed, but the cost of the intervention was high. Bangladesh was left deeply scarred, with a fractured society, a devastated economy, and a government struggling to reassert its legitimacy.

In the aftermath of the crisis, the military's role in the country's future became a subject of intense debate. Some called for the military to take a more active role in governance to ensure stability, while others warned against the dangers of prolonged military influence over civilian affairs. The legacy of the military's intervention would continue to shape the nation's political landscape for years to come.

In this chapter, we have examined the military's complex and controversial role in the 2024 crisis in Bangladesh. The army's actions, while instrumental in restoring order, also raised difficult questions about the balance of power between military and civilian authorities, the ethics of using force against one's own people, and the long-term prospects for peace and stability in the nation.

Chapter 9: A Nation Divided: The Social and Economic Impact

The political crisis of 2024 in Bangladesh left deep scars on the nation's social fabric and economic stability. This chapter explores how the turmoil reshaped society, widened existing divisions, and inflicted lasting damage on the economy, creating challenges that would take years to overcome.

Social Fragmentation: The Deepening of Divides

The conflict exacerbated pre-existing social divisions within Bangladesh, pitting different segments of society against one another. The unrest drew sharp lines between supporters of Sheikh Hasina's government and those aligned with the opposition, often leading to violent confrontations between communities. Families and neighborhoods, once united by shared history and culture, found themselves torn apart by political allegiances.

The role of the youth, particularly students, in leading the protests created a generational divide. Younger citizens, disillusioned by years of perceived government corruption and repression, clashed with older generations who were more likely to support the status quo. The involvement of students not only intensified the conflict but also left a lasting impact on the education system, with universities becoming battlegrounds and academic progress coming to a halt.

Ethnic and religious minorities, who often bore the brunt of government and military actions, faced increased marginalization and violence. The crisis fueled a rise in hate crimes and communal tensions, leaving these communities more vulnerable than ever. The social fabric of Bangladesh, once characterized by its diversity and resilience, was left frayed, with mistrust and fear replacing the bonds of solidarity.

Economic Devastation: The Cost of Conflict

The economic impact of the crisis was severe, affecting every sector of the economy. As protests turned into rebellion and then into a nationwide conflict, economic activity ground to a halt. The capital, Dhaka, once a bustling hub of commerce, saw its streets empty, businesses shuttered, and markets deserted. The violence and uncertainty drove away foreign investors, leading to a collapse in the stock market and a sharp decline in the value of the Bangladeshi Taka.

Key industries, including textiles and agriculture, were hit hard. The textile sector, a cornerstone of Bangladesh's economy and a major source of employment, faced massive disruptions. Factories closed, supply chains were severed, and international buyers pulled out of contracts due to the instability.

This led to widespread unemployment and left millions of workers, particularly women, without a source of income.

Agriculture, which provided livelihoods for a large portion of the rural population, was also severely affected. The fighting in rural areas, combined with disruptions in transportation and supply chains, led to food shortages and a spike in prices. Farmers, unable to access markets or secure their fields from the violence, saw their crops rot, further deepening the economic despair.

Humanitarian Crisis: Displacement and Despair

The prolonged conflict created a humanitarian crisis of unprecedented proportions. Hundreds of thousands of people were displaced, fleeing the violence in search of safety. Many sought refuge in makeshift camps, where conditions were dire, with limited access to food, clean water, and medical care.

The displacement crisis overwhelmed the government and humanitarian organizations, which were already stretched thin by the ongoing conflict.

The mental health toll on the population was immense. The constant fear of violence, the loss of loved ones, and the destruction of homes and livelihoods left deep psychological scars. The trauma of the conflict was particularly pronounced among children, who faced the disruption of their education, the loss of their homes, and exposure to violence.

The Breakdown of Institutions: Trust Eroded

The crisis also led to the breakdown of key state institutions. Public trust in the government, already low due to allegations of corruption and electoral fraud, eroded further as the crisis unfolded.

The government's heavy-handed response to the protests, its inability to protect citizens from violence, and its failure to address the root causes of the conflict all contributed to a deepening sense of disillusionment.

The judiciary, once seen as a pillar of fairness and justice, was perceived as compromised, with courts used to silence dissent rather than uphold the rule of law. The media, too, suffered under the weight of government censorship and control, losing its role as a watchdog and becoming a tool of propaganda.

The Long Road to Recovery: Rebuilding a Fractured Nation

As the conflict drew to a close, Bangladesh faced the daunting task of rebuilding. The path to recovery was fraught with challenges, including addressing the deep social divisions, revitalizing the economy, and restoring trust in institutions.

International aid and investment were critical in the initial stages of recovery, but the long-term success of rebuilding efforts depended on the political will to address the underlying issues that had led to the crisis.

Social reconciliation efforts, aimed at healing the wounds of the conflict, were initiated, but progress was slow. Truth and reconciliation commissions, peacebuilding initiatives, and community dialogue programs were established to foster understanding and rebuild trust among different segments of society.

Economically, the government launched a series of initiatives to revive key industries, attract foreign investment, and provide support to those hardest hit by the conflict. However, the road to economic recovery was long and fraught with obstacles, including continued political instability and the lingering effects of the crisis.

The Legacy of the 2024 Crisis

The 2024 crisis left an indelible mark on Bangladesh. The deep social and economic wounds it inflicted would take years, if not decades, to heal. The legacy of the conflict was one of a nation divided, struggling to overcome the scars of violence and rebuild in the face of immense challenges.

In this chapter, we have examined the profound social and economic impacts of the 2024 crisis in Bangladesh. The divisions it created, the destruction it wrought, and the humanitarian toll it exacted would shape the future of the nation, defining its path in the years to come. As Bangladesh looked to the future, it was clear that the journey toward healing and recovery would be long and arduous, requiring the collective efforts of all its people.

Chapter 10: International Outcry: Global Reactions and Diplomacy

The 2024 crisis in Bangladesh drew significant international attention, prompting a range of reactions from governments, international organizations, and civil society groups around the world. This chapter explores the global response to the unfolding events, highlighting how international pressure, diplomacy, and geopolitical interests shaped the course of the conflict and its aftermath.

Initial Reactions: A World Taken by Surprise

The initial protests in Bangladesh were largely seen as a domestic issue, and the international community, while concerned, did not immediately grasp the severity of the situation. However, as the violence escalated and reports of government crackdowns, human rights abuses, and the scale of the rebellion emerged, global attention sharply increased.

Human rights organizations were among the first to raise alarms. Groups like Amnesty International and Human Rights Watch issued urgent reports condemning the use of excessive force against protesters, the targeting of journalists, and the widespread arrests of political opponents. These reports quickly gained traction in global media, casting a harsh spotlight on Sheikh Hasina's government and sparking widespread condemnation.

The United Nations, through its human rights bodies and special rapporteurs, expressed deep concern over the situation. Calls for an immediate end to violence, protection of civilians, and respect for human rights were made, but these appeals initially fell on deaf ears as the conflict spiraled out of control.

Diplomatic Maneuvers: The Role of Neighboring Powers

As the crisis deepened, Bangladesh's regional neighbors, particularly India and China, became increasingly involved in diplomatic efforts. Both countries had significant strategic interests in Bangladesh, and the stability of the nation was crucial to their regional security and economic plans.

India, sharing a long border with Bangladesh and having deep historical ties, was particularly alarmed by the potential for the conflict to spill over into its own territory. The Indian government initially attempted to mediate, urging Sheikh Hasina to engage in dialogue with the opposition. However, as the situation worsened, India shifted its stance, providing behind-the-scenes support to the Bangladeshi government while also preparing for potential refugee flows and cross-border instability.

China, on the other hand, focused on protecting its investments and strategic interests in Bangladesh. Beijing offered diplomatic support to Sheikh Hasina's government, framing the crisis as an internal affair that should not be subject to foreign interference. China's stance was largely driven by its desire to maintain stability in the region and protect its Belt and Road Initiative projects in Bangladesh.

Both India and China faced criticism from the international community for their roles in the crisis, with many accusing them of prioritizing their strategic interests over the human rights of the Bangladeshi people.

Western Response: Sanctions and Condemnations

The Western response to the crisis was marked by a mix of condemnation, diplomatic pressure, and economic sanctions. The United States and European Union were vocal in their criticism of the Bangladeshi government's actions, with numerous statements condemning the violence and calling for an immediate ceasefire and the restoration of democratic processes.

In response to the human rights abuses, the U.S. and EU imposed targeted sanctions on key figures within the Bangladeshi government and military. These sanctions included asset freezes, travel bans, and restrictions on trade with entities linked to the government. The aim was to pressure Sheikh Hasina's regime to de-escalate the violence and engage in meaningful dialogue with the opposition.

However, the effectiveness of these sanctions was limited by the geopolitical realities of the region. Bangladesh's government, bolstered by support from China and reluctant to be seen as yielding to Western pressure, largely resisted the demands. The sanctions, while symbolically significant, did little to change the course of the conflict in the short term.

International Organizations: Humanitarian Response

As the crisis continued, international organizations, including the United Nations, the Red Cross, and various non-governmental organizations, mobilized to address the growing humanitarian crisis. These efforts focused on providing aid to displaced populations, ensuring access to food, water, and medical care, and advocating for the protection of civilians.

The UN Security Council held several emergency sessions to discuss the situation in Bangladesh, with member states divided over how to respond. While some countries pushed for a stronger interventionist approach, including the possibility of peacekeeping forces, others advocated for a diplomatic solution, fearing that foreign intervention could exacerbate the conflict.

Ultimately, the international community's ability to respond effectively was hampered by the complexity of the situation and the geopolitical interests at play. Humanitarian aid was often delayed or obstructed by ongoing violence and the government's reluctance to allow foreign organizations unfettered access to affected areas.

The Role of the Diaspora: Voices from Abroad

The Bangladeshi diaspora played a significant role in raising global awareness of the crisis. Activists, academics, and community leaders in countries with large Bangladeshi populations, such as the United Kingdom, the United States, and Canada, organized protests, lobbied their governments, and used social media to draw attention to the plight of those back home.

Diaspora groups were instrumental in shaping international perceptions of the crisis, framing it not just as a political conflict, but as a broader struggle for human rights and democracy in Bangladesh. Their efforts helped keep the issue in the global spotlight, ensuring that the crisis remained a topic of discussion in international forums.

Geopolitical Implications: A Shifting Landscape

The 2024 crisis in Bangladesh had significant geopolitical implications, altering the balance of power in South Asia and affecting relationships between major global powers. The conflict tested alliances, with countries forced to navigate a complex web of strategic interests, human rights concerns, and regional stability.

For Bangladesh, the crisis left the nation more isolated on the world stage, with its international reputation severely damaged. The government's actions during the conflict were widely condemned, and its relations with many Western nations were strained, leading to a period of diplomatic isolation.

At the same time, the crisis underscored the growing influence of China in South Asia, as Beijing's support for the Bangladeshi government demonstrated its willingness to back allies in the face of Western criticism.

This shift had long-term implications for the region, potentially realigning alliances and altering the strategic calculus of neighboring countries.

Conclusion: The Long Shadow of Global Reactions

The international outcry and diplomatic efforts during the 2024 crisis in Bangladesh highlighted the complexities of global governance in a world increasingly defined by geopolitical rivalries. While the international community's response was multifaceted, it was ultimately constrained by competing interests and the limitations of diplomatic and economic tools.

In this chapter, we have examined the global reactions to the crisis in Bangladesh, focusing on the interplay between diplomatic pressure, economic sanctions, and humanitarian efforts.

The international response, while significant, was unable to prevent the tragic escalation of violence, leaving a legacy of unresolved tensions and a nation deeply scarred by its experience on the global stage.

Chapter 11: The Path Forward: Rebuilding Bangladesh Post-Crisis

The 2024 crisis in Bangladesh left the nation facing the monumental task of rebuilding its society, economy, and political institutions. This chapter outlines the challenges and opportunities that lie ahead as Bangladesh embarks on the difficult journey of recovery and reconciliation, focusing on key areas such as political reform, economic revitalization, social cohesion, and the role of the international community in supporting these efforts.

Political Reform: Restoring Trust and Stability

The political landscape in Bangladesh was deeply fractured by the crisis, with trust in government institutions severely eroded. Rebuilding the nation requires significant political reform aimed at restoring faith in democracy and ensuring that the root causes of the conflict are addressed.

Key areas of focus include electoral reform, strengthening the judiciary, and ensuring freedom of the press.

Electoral reform is crucial for preventing future crises. The events of 2024 highlighted the need for a transparent and fair electoral process, free from manipulation and fraud. Establishing an independent electoral commission, implementing electronic voting systems, and introducing checks and balances to prevent abuse of power are essential steps in this direction.

Strengthening the judiciary is another critical component of political reform. To rebuild public trust, the judiciary must be seen as independent and impartial, capable of upholding the rule of law without interference from political forces.

Reforms should focus on ensuring judicial independence, reducing case backlogs, and increasing access to justice for all citizens.

Freedom of the press is vital for a functioning democracy, and efforts must be made to protect journalists and ensure a diverse and independent media landscape. The government should repeal repressive laws that curtail free speech, and promote a culture of open dialogue and transparency.

Economic Revitalization: Rebuilding a Shattered Economy

The economic impact of the crisis was devastating, with key industries disrupted, unemployment soaring, and investor confidence plummeting. Rebuilding the economy will require a multi-faceted approach that addresses both immediate needs and long-term development goals.

One of the first priorities is to revive the textile industry, which was heavily impacted by the conflict. This involves providing financial support to affected businesses, rebuilding supply chains, and restoring confidence among international buyers. Additionally, efforts should be made to diversify the economy, reducing reliance on textiles and exploring new growth sectors such as technology, agriculture, and tourism.

Reconstruction of infrastructure is another urgent need. The conflict left many areas with damaged roads, bridges, and public facilities, which are essential for economic recovery. The government, with support from international partners, must prioritize infrastructure projects that will create jobs, stimulate economic activity, and improve the quality of life for citizens.

To attract foreign investment, Bangladesh must work to restore investor confidence by ensuring political stability, implementing business-friendly policies, and enhancing the regulatory environment. International partnerships and trade agreements can also play a key role in driving economic growth.

Social Cohesion: Healing a Fractured Society

The social fabric of Bangladesh was deeply damaged by the 2024 crisis, with divisions along political, ethnic, and religious lines intensifying during the conflict. Rebuilding social cohesion will require a comprehensive approach that promotes reconciliation, addresses grievances, and fosters a sense of national unity.

Truth and reconciliation processes can help heal the wounds of the past by providing a platform for victims and perpetrators to share their experiences and seek justice.

These processes should be inclusive, transparent, and focused on restorative justice rather than retribution.

Education and community engagement are also crucial for rebuilding social cohesion. Educational programs that promote tolerance, diversity, and civic responsibility can help bridge divides and prevent future conflicts. Community dialogue initiatives, where people from different backgrounds can come together to discuss their concerns and build mutual understanding, should be encouraged and supported.

Addressing the needs of marginalized groups, including ethnic and religious minorities, women, and the poor, is essential for creating an inclusive society.

Policies that promote equal access to resources, opportunities, and representation in decision-making processes can help reduce inequalities and build a more just and cohesive society.

International Support: A Global Effort

The international community has a critical role to play in supporting Bangladesh's recovery. This support can take many forms, including financial aid, technical assistance, and diplomatic engagement.

Financial aid from international donors and institutions will be crucial for funding reconstruction efforts and supporting economic recovery. However, aid must be carefully managed to ensure it reaches those most in need and is used effectively to address the root causes of the crisis.

Technical assistance in areas such as governance, infrastructure development, and economic planning can help Bangladesh build the capacity needed to implement reforms and drive sustainable growth. International organizations, NGOs, and development agencies can provide expertise and resources to support these efforts.

Diplomatic engagement is also essential for ensuring that Bangladesh's recovery is supported by the global community. This includes advocating for human rights, promoting political stability, and encouraging international investment. The international community must remain committed to supporting Bangladesh as it navigates the challenges of post-crisis recovery.

Looking to the Future: A New Chapter for Bangladesh

The path forward for Bangladesh is fraught with challenges, but it also presents an opportunity to build a more resilient, inclusive, and democratic nation. The lessons learned from the 2024 crisis must inform the country's future, guiding efforts to prevent similar conflicts and ensuring that the nation emerges stronger and more united.

In this chapter, we have explored the key areas that Bangladesh must focus on as it rebuilds from the ashes of the crisis. Political reform, economic revitalization, social cohesion, and international support are all essential components of the recovery process. By addressing these challenges with determination and a commitment to justice and equity, Bangladesh can chart a new course toward a brighter and more prosperous future.

Chapter 12: Lessons from the Crisis: Implications for Global Democracy

The 2024 crisis in Bangladesh is not just a national tragedy but a cautionary tale with profound implications for global democracy. This chapter examines the lessons learned from the crisis, focusing on the vulnerabilities of democratic institutions, the role of civil society, the dangers of unchecked power, and the importance of international solidarity in preserving democratic values.

Erosion of Democratic Norms: A Global Concern
One of the most significant lessons from the 2024 crisis is the ease with which democratic norms can be eroded, even in countries with long histories of electoral politics. Bangladesh's descent into chaos was precipitated by a series of actions that undermined the integrity of its democratic institutions, particularly the electoral process.

The manipulation of the 2024 election, characterized by widespread fraud, voter intimidation, and the suppression of opposition voices, highlights the fragility of electoral democracy when checks and balances are weak or absent. This is a stark reminder for democracies worldwide that the safeguarding of free and fair elections is fundamental to the health of any democratic system. Electoral integrity must be protected through independent oversight, transparent processes, and robust legal frameworks that prevent abuse and ensure accountability.

The Role of Civil Society: A Double-Edged Sword

The crisis also underscores the critical role of civil society in both challenging and defending democracy. In Bangladesh, students and other civil society groups played a pivotal role in mobilizing against the government's actions, but their efforts were met with brutal repression.

This highlights the potential of civil society to act as a powerful force for change, but also the risks it faces when operating in hostile environments.

Globally, the Bangladesh crisis serves as a reminder of the need to protect and empower civil society organizations. Democracies must ensure that activists, journalists, and ordinary citizens have the space to express dissent without fear of retribution. At the same time, civil society must be vigilant in its efforts to hold those in power accountable, using tools such as advocacy, education, and nonviolent resistance.

Unchecked Power: The Dangers of Authoritarianism

The crisis in Bangladesh illustrates the dangers of unchecked executive power and the drift towards authoritarianism. Sheikh Hasina's government, emboldened by years of consolidating power, acted with impunity in the face of dissent, using state institutions to silence opposition and control the narrative.

This scenario is not unique to Bangladesh. Around the world, democratic backsliding is on the rise, with leaders in various countries undermining judicial independence, curtailing press freedom, and manipulating electoral processes to maintain their grip on power. The Bangladesh crisis serves as a warning that democracy must be actively defended against authoritarian tendencies. It emphasizes the need for strong institutions, an independent judiciary, and a free press as bulwarks against tyranny.

International Solidarity: The Need for Global Action

The international response to the Bangladesh crisis highlights both the potential and the limitations of global solidarity in defending democracy. While there was widespread condemnation and targeted sanctions from Western countries, these measures were insufficient to prevent the escalation of violence and the breakdown of democratic governance.

This raises important questions about the role of the international community in supporting democracies under threat. It underscores the need for more coordinated and effective international responses, including diplomatic pressure, economic incentives, and, when necessary, interventions to protect human rights and democratic norms. The crisis also reveals the importance of global networks of solidarity, where democratic nations, international organizations, and civil society groups work together to support and defend democratic values across borders.

A Call to Action: Strengthening Global Democracy

In the aftermath of the 2024 crisis in Bangladesh, it is clear that the global community must take proactive steps to strengthen democracy worldwide.

This includes supporting democratic transitions, promoting good governance, and building resilience against authoritarianism.

Educational initiatives that promote democratic values, civic engagement, and political participation are crucial for cultivating informed and active citizens who can hold their governments accountable. International efforts should also focus on supporting emerging democracies, providing them with the tools and resources needed to build strong, inclusive, and sustainable democratic institutions.

The crisis in Bangladesh is a sobering reminder that democracy is never guaranteed. It requires constant vigilance, active participation, and a commitment to the principles of justice, equality, and human rights. As the world reflects on the lessons of 2024, there is an urgent need for renewed dedication to protecting and advancing democracy, both in Bangladesh and around the globe.

Conclusion: The Legacy of 2024

The 2024 crisis in Bangladesh will be remembered as a pivotal moment in the country's history and a significant event in the global struggle for democracy. The lessons learned from this tragedy are not only relevant to Bangladesh but to all nations committed to the ideals of democratic governance.

In this chapter, we have explored the implications of the crisis for global democracy, focusing on the erosion of democratic norms, the role of civil society, the dangers of unchecked power, and the need for international solidarity. As Bangladesh begins the long process of recovery and rebuilding, the world must take these lessons to heart, ensuring that the legacy of 2024 is one of renewed commitment to the defense and promotion of democracy everywhere.